Colorful Puzzles for Wise Eyes

KEITH KAY

STERLING

New York / London
www.sterlingpublishing.com/kids

STERLING and the distinctive Sterling logo are registered trademarks
of Sterling Publishing Co., Inc.

10 9 8 7 6 5 4 3 2 1

Published by Sterling Publishing Co., Inc.
387 Park Avenue South, New York, NY 10016
© 2007 by Keith Kay
Distributed in Canada by Sterling Publishing
c/o Canadian Manda Group, 165 Dufferin Street
Toronto, Ontario, Canada M6K 3H6
Distributed in the United Kingdom by GMC Distribution Services
Castle Place, 166 High Street, Lewes, East Sussex, England BN7 1XU
Distributed in Australia by Capricorn Link (Australia) Pty. Ltd.
P.O. Box 704, Windsor, NSW 2756, Australia

Sterling ISBN-13: 978-1-4027-3277-5
ISBN-10: 1-4027-3277-5

For information about custom editions, special sales, premium and
corporate purchases, please contact Sterling Special Sales
Department at 800-805-5489 or specialsales@sterlingpub.com.

PUZZLES

◀ Can you see what's wrong with this jar of pickled onions?

WHAT KIND OF RING ISN'T ROUND?

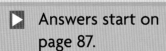 Answers start on page 87.

3

THIS CLOCK IS GOING ON STRIKE!

▲ A clock strikes 6:00 in 5 seconds. Does it take twice as long to strike 12:00?

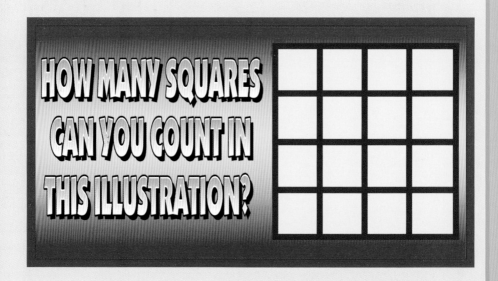

HOW MANY SQUARES CAN YOU COUNT IN THIS ILLUSTRATION?

IF YOU WERE RUNNING IN A RACE AND YOU PASSED THE PERSON IN SECOND PLACE, WHAT PLACE WOULD YOU BE IN?

WHAT'S WRONG WITH THIS WATCH?

In the English language, is it ever grammatically correct to say "I is"?

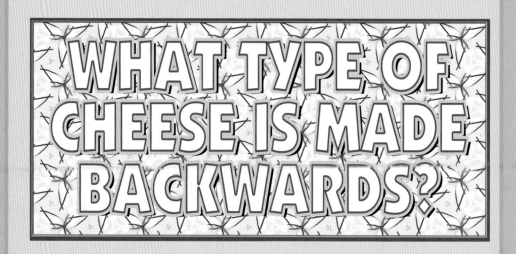

WHAT TYPE OF CHEESE IS MADE BACKWARDS?

WHAT'S WRONG WITH THIS PICTURE?

XI+I=X

△ The solution to this mathematical equation is incorrect as written. How can you make it right?

HOW CAN YOU ADD 2 TO 11 TO MAKE 1?

△ When you take 2 apples from 3 apples, what do you have?

If five spiders can catch five flies in 5 minutes, how many spiders are required to catch a hundred flies in 100 minutes?

Can you say this phrase 10 times very quickly?

▲ There is only one word in the English language that ends in the letters AMT. Can you name the word?

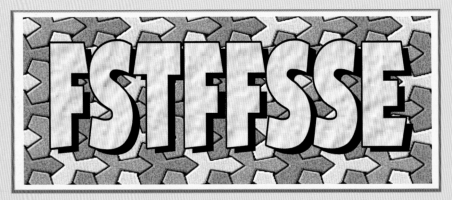

△ What are the next two letters that will come in the sequence after the letter E?

backwards
sdrawkcab
backwards
sdrawkcab

Name three sporting events in which the event is won by competitors that go backwards.

WHAT CAN YOU PUT IN A GLASS BOTTLE, BUT NEVER TAKE OUT OF IT?

Can you say
"ROBERT AND RICHARD
PURCHASED A RETRIEVER"
without sounding the R's?

FRIDAY
13

IF FRIDAY IS TWO DAYS BEFORE
THE DAY BEFORE YESTERDAY,
WHAT DAY IS IT TODAY?

WHAT IS THIS CHRISTMAS GREETING?

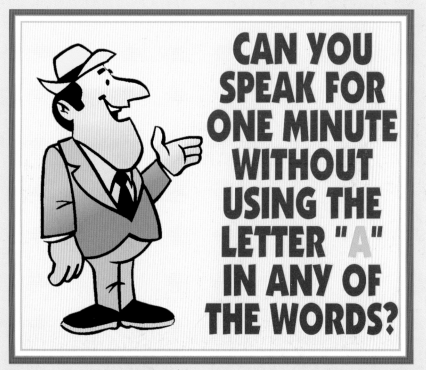

CAN YOU SPEAK FOR ONE MINUTE WITHOUT USING THE LETTER "A" IN ANY OF THE WORDS?

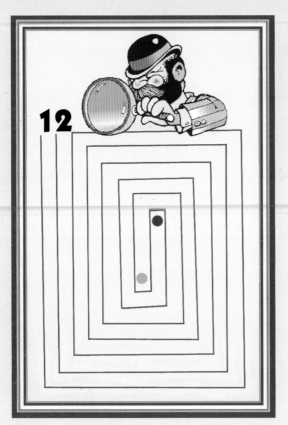

Using just your eyes, can you figure out which path leads to the red dot? Is it 1 or 2?

12

TOM IS TWICE AS OLD AS JOHN
WAS WHEN TOM WAS AS OLD
AS JOHN IS NOW.
TOM IS NOW 24.
HOW OLD IS JOHN?

WHAT IS ALWAYS COMING BUT NEVER ARRIVES?

The cavalier can't find the spy. Can you?

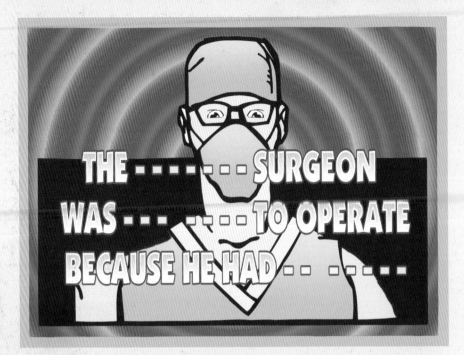

THE - - - - - - - SURGEON
WAS - - - - - - - TO OPERATE
BECAUSE HE HAD - - - - - - -

Fill in the 7 blank spaces between words. In each case, the same 7 letters are used and they are in the same sequence, yet each missing word or phrase is pronounced in a different way. What are the 7 letters?

A FARMER HAS 2 FRESH EGGS FOR BREAKFAST EVERY DAY. HE HAS NO HENS; HE DOESN'T TRADE, BUY, OR STEAL THEM, AND HE DOESN'T HAVE THEM GIVEN TO HIM. SO WHERE DOES HE GET THE EGGS FROM?

If you pronounce GH as in "tough," O as in "women," and TI as in "lotion," how do you pronounce GHOTI?

What's the opposite of NOT IN?

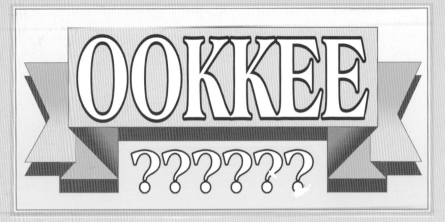

△ Put a letter at the front and 3 letters at the end of the sequence of letters shown to make an everyday word.

△ Name a word that starts and ends with the letters HE. Then name another one.

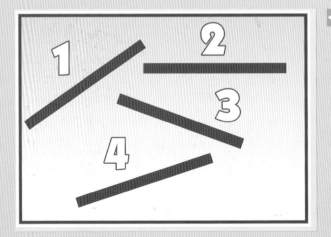

◁ Using just your eyes, which line is the shortest?

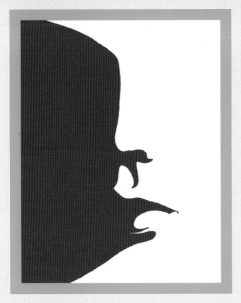

EXCEL
CUTIE
ESSAY
EMPTY
EASY
ELLEN

▲ What do you see? If a few extra bits and pieces were added, they would make it obvious. Any ideas?

▲ All these words have something in common. What is it?

THE VORACIOUS VULTURES

▲ There were 3 vultures on a branch. A hunter shot and killed one. How many vultures were left on the branch?

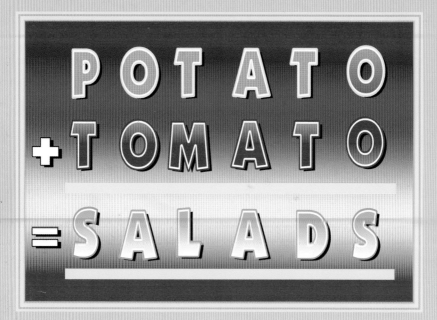

POTATO
+ TOMATO
= SALADS

▲ Each letter stands for a different number. Can you do this sum? To start you off, the letter O = 4.

▲ This design is composed of all the letters of the alphabet. Can you find all 26?

USING THE WORDS NEWS & DROVES WRITE SEVEN WORDS USING EACH LETTER ONCE.

Two babies were born within minutes of each other on the same day, in the same hospital, and of the same parents, but they were not twins. Can you explain this?

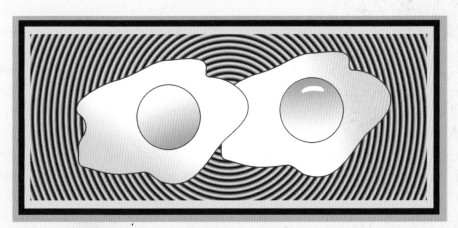

Which is correct: "The yolks of eggs is white" or "The yolks of eggs are white"?

CAN YOU NAME FOUR DAYS OF THE WEEK THAT START WITH THE LETTER T?

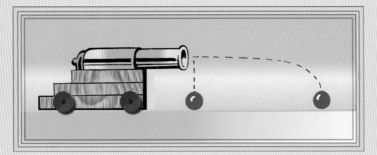

▲ If a cannon ball is shot half a mile horizontally and another is dropped from the same point simultaneously as shown above, which will hit the ground first?

▲ What letter comes next in the above sequence?

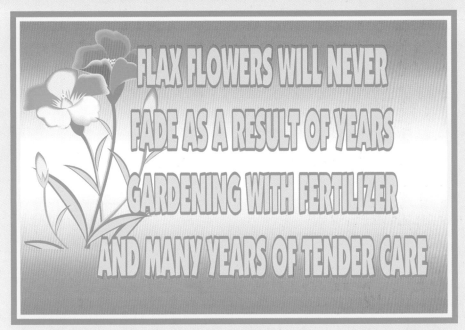

FLAX FLOWERS WILL NEVER FADE AS A RESULT OF YEARS GARDENING WITH FERTILIZER AND MANY YEARS OF TENDER CARE

Using just your eyes, how many times does the letter F appear in the above phrase?

VOLIX

How do you pronounce the phrase written above? Think about it.

▲ Two puzzles: 1. A brick weighs 1 pound + half a brick. How much does a brick and a half weigh?
2. Using just your eyes, are these bricks laid in perfectly straight lines?

◀ Can you work out what word these arrows represent?

WHAT'S IN THE BOX?

▲ It has a head and a tail, but it has no legs or body.

◀ Brothers and sisters I have none, but this man's father is my father's son. Who is he?

1 2 3
4 5 ?

▲ Study this set of shapes. Can you work out the shape that will replace the question mark?

▲ A pond has a single water lily, and the number of water lilies on the pond doubles every day. After 14 days, they cover the entire area of the pond. How many days did it take to cover half the area?

Hidden somewhere in this mosaic design is a 5-pointed star. Can you find it?

WHAT WORD CAN BE WRITTEN BACKWARDS OR FORWARDS OR UPSIDE DOWN AND CAN STILL BE READ FROM LEFT TO RIGHT?

THE SEQUOIA TREE

▲ What's unusual about the word SEQUOIA?

TBoNtBt - - -

▲ What are the next 3 letters in the above sequence?

NEW DOOR

▲ Rearrange the letters of NEW DOOR to make just one word.

△ What everyday word is represented by this sequence of letters?

◄ The vowels have been removed from the name of this well-known vegetable. Which vegetable is it?

△ Repeat this tongue-twister 10 times very quickly. Try not to say "stinking" or "stunk."

I SHAVE ONLY THOSE WHO DO NOT SHAVE THEMSELVES

▲ This sign was in the barber's window. Does the barber shave himself?

THE BLIND PIG PUZZLE

▲ Spell the words BLIND PIG with just six letters.

◀ Can you rearrange these letters to form a word?

JFMAKMJJASOND

▲ Which one of these 13 letters does not belong to the sequence?

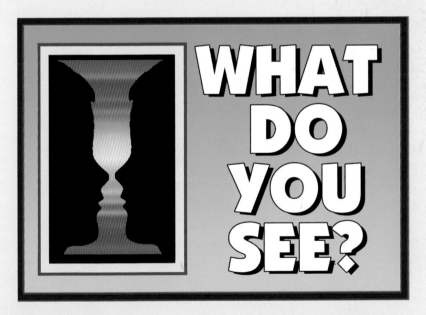

WHAT DO YOU SEE?

▲ Is this a goblet or vase, or two faces looking at each other?

st   nd   rd

▲ Here are two puzzles in one.
1. Insert the same letter in each of the two blank spaces to make a word.
2. What can you place in front of each pair of letters to make the sequence readable and logical?

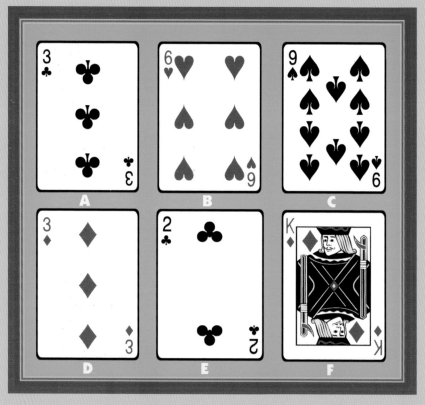

▲ Can you spot 5 mistakes in these six cards?

▲ Stare at the small red dot for about 30 seconds. Try not to blink. Then transfer your gaze to a sheet of white paper or a blank wall. Who do you see?

◀ There is only one 4-letter word that ends in ENY. Can you name it?

A PIG'S TALE

FIVE PIGS ARE STANDING IN A STRAIGHT LINE, NOSE TO TAIL. HOW MANY OF THE PIGS ARE ABLE TO SAY THAT ANOTHER PIG'S TAIL IS TOUCHING ITS NOSE?

Rearrange these letters to make a new word.

There are two swans in front of a swan, two swans behind a swan, and a swan in the middle. How many swans are there?

WHICH IS LONGER, THE HAT'S BRIM OR ITS HEIGHT? GUESS FIRST, THEN MEASURE.

IT'S AS LIGHT AS A FEATHER, BUT EVEN A STRONG MAN CAN'T HOLD IT FOR MUCH LONGER THAN A MINUTE. WHAT IS IT?

AUG

These are the three middle letters of a common 5-letter word. Can you name it?

▲ What are the next three letters to complete the sequence?

▲ Moving just one glass, can you change things so that the glasses alternate between empty and full ones?

▲ Can you work out what word this is? Clue: The dots are missing from the i's.

I have two coins in my hand. Their total value is 15 cents, but one of the coins is not a dime. What are the two coins?

The more of these you put in a wheelbarrow, the lighter the wheelbarrow becomes. What are they?

A FARMER HAD 17 SHEEP. ALL BUT 9 DIED. HOW MANY WERE STILL ALIVE?

NINE THUMPS

▲ If you gave someone nine thumps, what might you expect to receive in return? Rearrange the letters for the answer.

WHAT CAN YOU LOOK THROUGH, BUT NOT SEE THROUGH?

·OO ·A·Y ·OO··
··OI· ··E ··O··

▲ Can you identify this proverb? The consonants have been removed. Only the vowels are showing.

WHAT PAT CHAT THAT FAT BAT CAT RAT

▲ Which of these 8 words is the odd one out?

▲ Take two identical sheets of paper. Label one LIGHT and the other HEAVY. Hold one sheet in each hand, at the same height, and let them drop to the floor. How can you ensure that the one labeled HEAVY lands on the floor first?

◄ What does this shape represent?

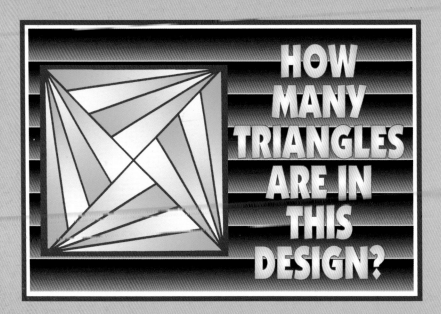

HOW MANY TRIANGLES ARE IN THIS DESIGN?

▲ Without cutting the paper, can you make the parrot go into the cage?

THROUGH
BOUGH
COUGH
DOUGH
ROUGH

◀ What's unusual about these 5 words?

W
WAW
WASAW
WASISAW
WASITISAW
WASITATISAW
WASITACATISAW
WASITATISAW
WASITISAW
WASISAW
WASAW
WAW
W

◀ Study these letters very carefully. How many times do you think it says "Was it a cat I saw"? You can read it up, down, left, and right, and follow a straight or winding path; you can even reuse letters.

▲ What does the red shape represent?

▲ This shape is part of a sign many people see almost every day. What is the sign?

I can be ...

WRITTEN
SPOKEN
EXPOSED
BROKEN

What am I?

THEIR IS FIVE ERRERS IN THIS SENTANCE

▲ Can you find the errors?

IF PETER'S FATHER IS DAVID'S SON, WHAT RELATION IS PETER TO DAVID?

3 6 13 26 33 ?

▲ What number completes the sequence?

OWL
DOVE
FINCH
ROBIN
EAGLE
OSTRICH

WHICH OF THESE BIRDS IS THE ODD ONE OUT?

CROSSWORD PUZZLE

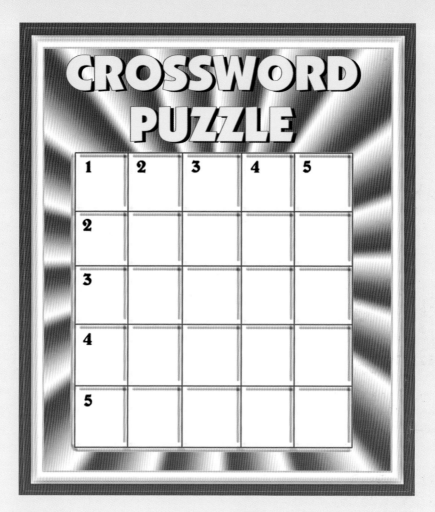

1	2	3	4	5
2				
3				
4				
5				

Across

1. Command from a librarian
2. Tranquility
3. Like a soundproofed room
4. Peace and _____
5. Make less agitated

Down

1. Some equipment for playing pool
2. Take advantage of
3. Parts of needles or potatoes
4. Freedom from pain or difficulty
5. Golf balls rest on them

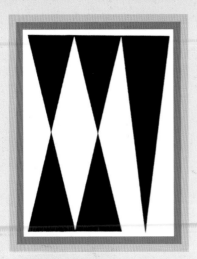

Why was this used as the logo for the 25th Anniversary of the Museum of Modern Art in New York?

There's one in COW, two in WOW and three in BOW-WOW, so how many W's are there in total?

I START WITH THE LETTER E.
I END WITH THE LETTER E.
I CONTAIN ONLY ONE LETTER,
YET I AM NOT THE LETTER E.
WHAT AM I?

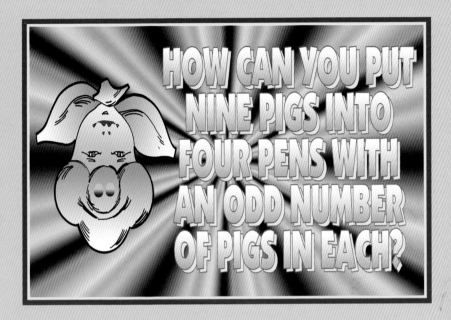

HOW CAN YOU PUT NINE PIGS INTO FOUR PENS WITH AN ODD NUMBER OF PIGS IN EACH?

YES

▲ To what question can you never answer YES?

IF 2's COMPANY & 3's A CROWD, WHAT'S 4 AND 5?

IT HAS A MOUTH BUT IT CANNOT SPEAK. IT HAS A BED, YET IT NEVER SLEEPS, WHAT IS IT?

1000
20
30
1000
1030
1000
20

Cover the numbers with a piece of paper, leaving the top 1000 visible. Slowly scroll the piece of paper down the page, counting aloud and adding each number to the total as it is revealed. When you include the last number, what is the grand total? Are you sure?

How many garden tools can you find?

▲ What's strange about this arrangement of numbers?

WHAT COAT IS ALWAYS WET WHEN YOU PUT IT ON?

▲ Is this 3 blue squares in a yellow oblong, or is it something else?

NEST
ACHE
DRUM

▲ The same 3-letter word can be placed in front of each of the above words to form a new word. Can you figure out what the 3-letter word is?

How much earth is there in a hole 3 feet wide and 4 feet deep?

LIG HTUP WIT HAFLA SHOFINS PIRATI ON!

What does this sequence of letters mean?

ERGRO

▲ Look at these letters. If you place 3 letters before them and the same 3 letters after them, you will make an everyday word. What is the word?

ROYGBI

▲ What is the next letter in this sequence?

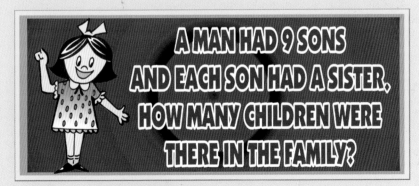

A MAN HAD 9 SONS AND EACH SON HAD A SISTER. HOW MANY CHILDREN WERE THERE IN THE FAMILY?

CAN A MAN MARRY HIS WIDOW'S NIECE?

CRABCAKE
CANOPY
CALMNESS
DEFT
FIRST
HIJACK
LAUGHING
STUPID

◀ Can you see what's unusual about these words?

CAN YOU SPOT THE DIFFERENCE?

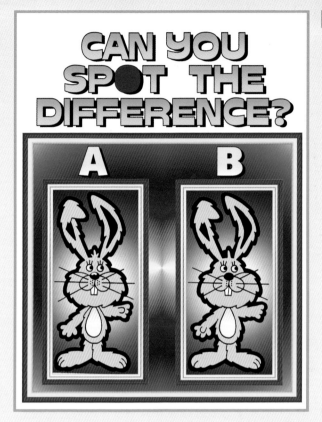

A   B

There are nine small differences in picture B, compared to picture A. Can you find them?

Hold the book at eye level. Look down the page in the direction of the arrow. Which famous fictional character can you see? The answer is really elementary.

A glass marble is placed inside a glass bottle. A cork is inserted as a stopper. How can you get the marble out of the bottle without pulling the cork out or smashing the bottle?

What well-known phrase or saying has been hidden in this strange design?

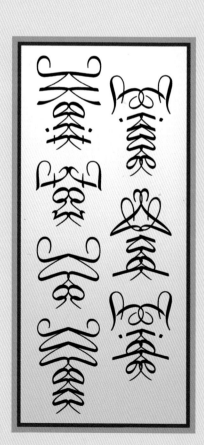

▲ Where is the king of the castle hiding? Can you find him?

◄ Can you find the rustler?

WANTED

How many times do the hour and minute hands of a clock cross each other in the 12-hour period between 5:00 p.m. and 5:00 a.m.?

HOW MANY TIMES CAN YOU SUBTRACT THE NUMBER 7 FROM THE NUMBER 42?

▲ Who or what is this?

▲ Five postage stamps are placed loose on a table. How can you blow on them so that only the white stamp remains on the table?

yYHₗyEyт

▲ What are the next four letters in this series?

▲ This is a copy of a genuine postage stamp. The artist made a small mistake in the design. Where did the artist go wrong?

▲ Here are two puzzles in one. 1. How far can a dog chase a rabbit into a forest? 2. Can you change this rabbit to another animal?

▲ Which burns longer, a candle made of wax or one made of tallow?

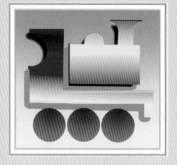

◀ Imagine you are an engine driver. At your first stop of the day, you pick up 45 passengers. At the next stop, you pick up 12 and drop off 17 passengers. At your next stop you pick up 24 and drop off 39. What is the name of the engine driver?

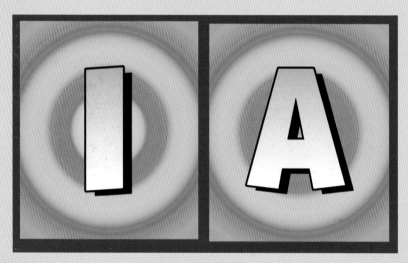

▲ A 4-letter word starts with the letter I. If you now add a letter A to the start, the word's pronunciation is unchanged. What is the word?

◀ What do these shapes mean? Try to discover the secret by looking at this page from different angles.

1 AIMOUVWXY

2 BCDEIKOX

▲ Here's an easy puzzle to reflect on. Can you see what all the letters in set 1 have in common? Now look at set 2. What do these letters have in common? There is one other letter that could be added to either set. Can you name it?

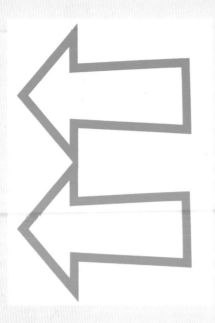

◀ Can you make a third arrow by adding just two lines?

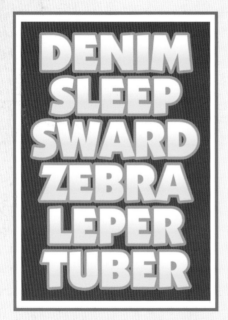

DENIM
SLEEP
SWARD
ZEBRA
LEPER
TUBER

▲ Which of these words is the odd one out?

▲ Who is the tallest man: 1, 2, or 3?

NANA NENE NINI NONO

▲ Mary's father had five daughters. The first four were Nana, Nene, Nini, and Nono. What was the fifth daughter called?

◀ What do these shapes depict?

What do these shapes represent?

WHAT IS IT THAT BELONGS TO YOU, BUT WHICH OTHERS USE MORE THAN YOU DO?

◀ What's wrong with this picture?

◀ How many English words can you name that rhyme with the ones in this list?

ORANGE
MORGUE
MONTH
BULB
SCARCE
PURPLE
SILVER

▲ What time is it?

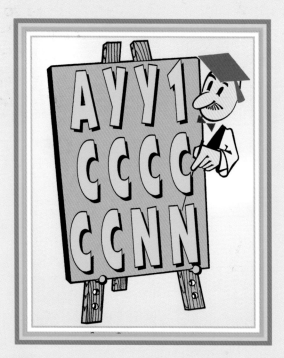

▲ Can you read this phrase?

◀ Place 12 coins or buttons so there are 4 on each side as shown. Now rearrange them to form a square with 5 on each side.

◀ If you only have one match and you go into a dark room in which there is a candle, an oil lamp, and a fire, what should you light first?

▲ Are these perfect circles?

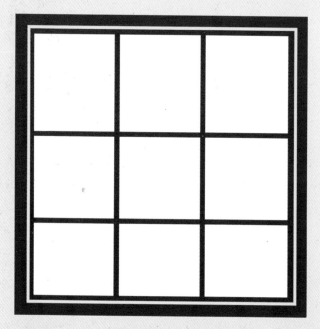

▲ Place the numbers 1 to 9 in the boxes so that each line (across, down, or diagonal) adds up to 15.

◀ Some months have 30 days, others have 31 days. How many months have 28 days?

▲ Here are two puzzles in one. 1. Write down the name of a famous person (living or dead). With my magic powers, regardless of what you have written down, if you turn to page 95 you will see that I have written exactly the same. 2. Does the frame shown get narrower toward the right side?

▲ Can you tell what
creature this is?

▲ Can you find the two children
hiding in these flowers?

When a wealthy king died, he left 17 horses to his 3 sons. The first son was to be given half of them; the next son, a third; and the youngest, a ninth. How did they divide the horses?

"I AM LOOKING FOR YOU"

How can you abbreviate this text message into just three letters?

A frog is at the bottom of a 90-foot well. Each hour it climbs up 3 feet and slips back 2 feet. How many hours will it take the frog to get out?

Can you name the next three letters?

You have 10 green and 10 blue mittens in a drawer. In complete darkness, how many mittens would you need to pull out to get a matching pair of the same color?

WHERE IS THE BOY HIDING?

▲ Can you find him?

▲ Why is the letter A
like a flower?

WHAT GOES UP
A CHIMNEY
DOWN, BUT
WON'T COME
DOWN A
CHIMNEY UP?

1

ORANGE BLUE YELLOW
GREEN RED BLACK
RED YELLOW PURPLE
BLACK GREEN ORANGE
PURPLE RED BLUE
ORANGE BLUE GREEN

2

ORANGE BLUE YELLOW
GREEN RED BLACK
RED YELLOW PURPLE
BLACK GREEN ORANGE
PURPLE RED BLUE
ORANGE BLUE GREEN

 In section 1, read aloud the name of the color of ink that has been used to write each word. Now try to do the same in section 2: name aloud the color of ink, NOT the word that is spelled. You will find it very difficult.

 How many kinds of animals did Moses take into the ark?

WHAT IS IN SEASONS, SECONDS, CENTURIES, AND MINUTES, BUT NOT IN DECADES, YEARS OR DAYS?

▲ What do these shapes mean? Can you read the words?

▲ For this puzzle, use 20 small drinking straws. Can you arrange them to make a 10-letter word without bending or breaking any of the straws?

▲ This is a well-known proverb. Only the vowels are shown. Can you fill in the blanks?

▲ Here are two puzzles in one. 1. A doctor gives you three pills and tells you to swallow one every half-hour. How long will the supply of pills last? 2. How can you pop the pill into the monk's mouth?

▲ What's the last thing you take off before you get into bed?

WHAT ALWAYS ENDS EVERYTHING?

KID GLOVES
DICE GAMBLE
BEECH NUTS
CHOICE QUALITY
COOKBOOK PAGES

▲ Look at the reflection of this page in a mirror. Now turn the book upside down and look at this page again in the mirror. What happens and why?

THE BIGGER FAMILY

◄ Who is the biggest member of this family? Is it Mr. Bigger, Mrs. Bigger, or their child, Ruth?

▲ Can you figure out what these dark shapes are?

◀ Stare at the dot for about 30 seconds. Try not to blink. Now look at a piece of white paper or a blank wall. Who do you see?

WHICH MEMBER OF THE BRITISH ROYAL FAMILY WEARS THE BIGGEST CROWN?

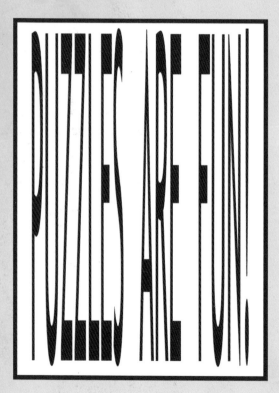

◀ What do these shapes mean?

ANSWERS

Page 3
(*top, left*) The neck is too small. It would be impossible to put the onions into the jar.
(*bottom, right*) A boxing ring.

Page 4
(*top*) The clock takes 11 seconds to strike 12:00, so it's more than twice as long as striking 6:00.
(*bottom*) 30.

Page 5
(*top*) Second place.
(*middle*) The Roman numerals for 9 and 11 are reversed.
(*bottom*) Yes. Example: "I is the first letter of the word ink."

Page 6
(*top*) Edam.
(*bottom*) The grapevine has the wrong type of leaves.

Page 7
(*top*) Turn the page upside down. The equation is now correct: X = I + IX.

(*middle*) It's all to do with time. If you add 2 hours to 11 o'clock, you get 1 o'clock.
(*bottom*) You have two apples.

Page 8
(*top*) Five spiders.
(*bottom*) You may get it wrong because it's a tongue twister.

Page 9
(*top*) DREAMT.
(*bottom*) Turn the page upside down.

Page 10
(*top*) A towel.
(*middle*) NT. The letters are the initial letters of First, Second, Third, etc., so the next ones are Ninth and Tenth.
(*bottom*) Two. There was one continuous groove on each side.

Page 11
(*top*) Rowing, backstroke (swimming), and tug of war.
(*bottom*) Cracks.

Page 12

(*top*) Bob and Dick bought a dog.
(*bottom*) Tuesday.

Page 13

(*top*) NOEL (No L). The letter L is missing from the sequence.
(*bottom*) Count aloud the numbers from 1 to 1000.

Page 14

(*top*) It's number 2.
(*bottom*) 18.

Page 15

(*top*) Tomorrow.
(*bottom*) Turn the page upside down. The outline of his head can be seen in the lower right.

Page 16

(*top*) NOTABLE. The NOTABLE surgeon was NOT ABLE to operate because he had NO TABLE.
(*bottom*) Ducks. They were ducks' eggs.

Page 17

(*top*) FISH.
(*bottom*) IN.

Page 18

(*top*) BOOKKEEPER.
(*middle*) Heartache and headache.
(*bottom*) Number 3.

Page 19

(*top, left*) A face. Add the eyes and eyebrows.

(*top, right*) Each word can be expressed in just 2 letters. EXAMPLES: XL QT SA.
(*bottom*) None; the other 2 flew away.

Page 20

(*top*)   345954
        +   546954
            892908

(*bottom*) Seek and you will find!

Page 21

(*top*) SEVEN WORDS.
(*middle*) They were part of a set of triplets.
(*bottom*) Neither is correct because the yolks of eggs are yellow.

Page 22

(*top*) Tuesday, Thursday, today, and tomorrow.

(*middle*) Both would touch the level ground at the same moment, because the force of gravity is not affected by the horizontal projection and speed of the ball being shot.

(*bottom*) The letter S, the first letter of Sequence, comes next. The letters are the first letters of "What Letter Comes Next In The Above...."

Page 23

(*top*) There are 6 F's in the phrase. Many people miss the F's in the two instances of the word "of."

(*bottom*) Volume 9.

Page 24

(*top*) 1. 3 lbs. 2. Yes, the bricks are in perfectly straight lines across.

(*bottom*) NEWS. The arrows are pointing North, East, West, and South.

Page 25

(*top*) A coin.

(*bottom*) The speaker's son.

Page 26

(*top*) The number 6 and its mirror image.

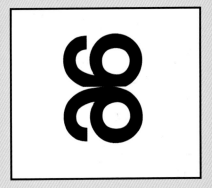

(*bottom*) 13 days.

Page 27

(*top*)

(*bottom*) NOON.

Page 28

(*top*) SEQUOIA is the shortest word that contains the vowels A, E, I, O, and U.

(*middle*) ITQ. The sequence is the initial letters of the words, "To be or not to be, that is the question," a well-known quotation from Shakespeare's *Hamlet*.

(*bottom*) Just rearrange the letters to spell. ONE WORD.

Page 29

(*top*) Water (H_2O or H to O).

(*middle*) Onion.

Page 30

(*top*) There is no answer to this question. It's a paradox.

(*bottom*) BLNDPG. A blind pig has no use for its eyes (I's).

Page 31

(*top*) EUREKA.

(*middle*) The letter K. Without the K, the sequence shows the first letter of each month of the year.

(*bottom*) The choice is yours!

Page 32

(*top*) Insert the letter A to make the word "standard." Insert the numerals 1, 2, and 3 to make 1st, 2nd, and 3rd.

(*bottom*) 3 of Clubs: The top center club should be the other way up. 6 of Hearts: No mistakes on this one. 9 of Spades: The card shows 10 pips. There is one spade too many. 3 of Diamonds: The bottom 3 has been reversed. 2 of Clubs: The tails have been cut off the central clubs. Last card: This is marked as the King of Diamonds but the drawing shows a Jack.

Page 33

(*top*) Ex-President Bill Clinton and the flag in the background will appear in their true colors.

(*bottom*) DENY.

Page 34

(*top*) None of them. Pigs can't talk!

(*bottom*) SLEEPLESSNESS.

Page 35

(*top*) Three swans.

(*bottom*) They are both the same size, but most people see the height as longer.

Page 36

(*top*) Breath.

(*bottom*) LAUGH.

Page 37

(*top*) ENT for Eight, Nine, Ten. The sequence is formed from the first letters of One, Two, Three, etc.

(*middle*) Pour the contents of glass 2 into glass 5.
(*bottom*) minimum.

Page 38
(*top*) The two coins are a dime and a nickel One of the coins wasn't a dime, but the other coin was.
(*bottom*) Holes.

Page 39
(*top*) Nine.
(*bottom*) PUNISHMENT.

Page 40
(*top*) A book.
(*middle*) Too many cooks spoil the broth.
(*bottom*) The odd one out is WHAT. Although each word ends in AT, WHAT is the only one that does not rhyme with any of the other words.

Page 41
(*top*) Crumple the paper labeled HEAVY into a ball. When dropped, it's bound to hit the floor first.
(*bottom*) It's a capital or upper-case letter E, drawn in a shadow typeface.

Page 42
(*top*) 56.
(*bottom*) Slowly bring the page closer to your face. Aim to let your nose touch the small dot. At a certain distance, the parrot will appear to go into the cage.

Page 43
(*top*) All the words end in OUGH, but those letters are pronounced in a different way in each word.
(*bottom*) According to puzzle expert Sam Loyd, there are 63,504 ways.

Page 44
(*top*) It's a capital letter S.
(*bottom*) It's part of the EXIT sign.

Page 45

(*top*) The news.

(*bottom*) THEIR should be THERE, IS should be ARE, ERRERS should be ERRORS, SENTANCE should be SENTENCE, and the final error: there are only 4 errors, not 5. There are 4 mistakes not counting the word "FIVE." But if FIVE is a mistake, then there really are 5 errors. In which case FIVE isn't an error and there are only 4 errors....

Page 46

(*top*) David is Peter's grandfather.

(*middle*) 66. 3 is doubled to make 6, +7 = 13, which is doubled to make 26, +7 = 33, etc.

(*bottom*) The ostrich. It's the only one that can't fly.

Page 47

Across: All the answers are QUIET. Down: 1, Q's (cues). 2, U's (use). 3, I's (eyes). 4, E'S (ease). 5, T's (tees).

Page 48

(*top*) The shapes represent the number 25 in Roman numerals, XXV.

(*middle*) There are no W's in the word TOTAL.

(*bottom*) An envelope.

Page 49

(*top*)

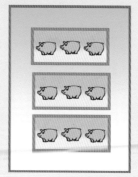

(*bottom*) Are you asleep?

Page 50

(*top*) 9.

(*bottom*) A river.

Page 51

(*top*) It's 4,100, not 5,000.

(*bottom*) Nine: flowerpot, pitchfork, clippers, shears, spade, roller, trowel, watering can, wheelbarrow.

Page 52

(*top*) It's a magic square. Each horizontal, vertical, and diagonal line adds up to 24. So does each group of 4 corner squares. What makes it unusual is that it also works when the page is turned upside down.

(*bottom*) A coat of paint.

Page 53

(*top*) It's a letter E.

(*bottom*) EAR.

Page 54
(*top*) There is no earth in a hole of any size!

(*bottom*) The words have had their spacing changed. They should read: LIGHT UP WITH A FLASH OF INSPIRATION.

Page 55
(*top*) UNDERGROUND.

(*middle*) The next is V for violet. The sequence shows the first letter of each color in the rainbow (red, orange, yellow, green, blue, and indigo).

(*bottom*) Ten. The nine boys had just one sister.

Page 56
(*top*) No. He'd be dead.

(*bottom*) Each word contains a sequence of letters that are in consecutive order. For example, CALMNESS has LMN. CANOPY has NOP. Can you think of any other words that have this property?

Page 57
(*top*) Here are the nine differences. In picture B: Rabbit's right ear is missing a line. Rabbit's left eye has one eyelash missing. Highlight on nose is filled in. Part of lowest right whisker is missing. Cheek line under right eye is missing. Right paw is different. Toe line is missing from right foot. Rabbit's left thumb is missing. Extra dots under nose missing. Note: "Left" refers to the rabbit's left, which is on your right.

(*bottom*) Sherlock Holmes.

Page 58
(*top*) Push the cork *into* the bottle so it falls inside. The marble will then roll out when you tip the bottle.

(*bottom*) Turn the page 90 degrees counterclockwise. Look carefully and you will see it says Time And Tide Wait For No Man. You can see the phrase and the mirror reflection of the phrase.

Page 59
(*top*) Turn the page 90 degrees clockwise. His face is formed from the skyline.

(*bottom*) Rotate the page 90 degrees counterclockwise. His face can be seen between the steer's two ears.

Page 60
(*top*) The hands will cross each other eleven times at the following (approximate) times: 5:27, 6:32, 7:38, 8:43, 9:49, 10:54, 12:00, 1:05, 2:10, 3:16, and 4:21.

(*bottom*) Once, because after that you are no longer subtracting from 42.

Page 61

(*top*) George Washington. View the page from a long distance.
(*bottom*) Place your finger on the white stamp as you start to blow!

Page 62

(*top*) RRRR, for SeptembeR, OctobeR, NovembeR, DecembeR. The letters are taken from the last letter of each month: JanuarY, FebruarY, etc.
(*bottom*) The locomotive's wheels have no connecting rods.

Page 63

(*top*) 1. Halfway. After that it is running out of the forest. 2. The rabbit changes into a duck if you turn the page 90 degrees counterclockwise.
(*bottom*) Neither. Candles don't burn longer, they burn shorter! Note that if you look at the candles, each can also be seen as two profile faces.

Page 64

(*top*) It's your name.
(*bottom*) ISLE. It becomes AISLE.

Page 65

(*top*) It's the number 5 (turn the page 90 degrees clockwise).

(*bottom*) The letters directly under number 1 are all legible if you look at the reflection of the page in a mirror. Those under number 2 are readable in a mirror if the page is turned upside down. The letter that could be placed in either set of letters is H.

Page 66

(*top*)

(*bottom, left*) ZEBRA. All the words form another word when reversed, e.g. DENIM changes to MINED, SWARD to DRAWS, etc. This is not possible with ZEBRA.
(*bottom, right*) Man 1 is the tallest. This is not the standard perspective illusion, in which all three are the same size.

Page 67

(*top*) Mary.
(*bottom*) Turn the page 90 degrees counterclockwise; you'll see a man's head.

Page 68

(*top*) The number 2.
(*bottom*) Your name.

Page 69

(*top*) Roosters do not have webbed feet.

(*bottom*) None of these words have rhyming words, unless you know differently!

Page 70

(*top*) 12:55, or 5 minutes to 1:00 (5 to 1).

(*bottom*) A wise one foresees seasons.

Page 71

(*top*)

(*bottom*) The match.

Page 72

(*top*) Yes, they are perfect circles; trace one out with a compass to check.

(*bottom*)

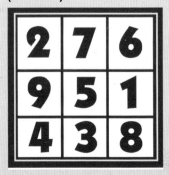

Page 73

(*top*) Every month has 28 days.

(*bottom*) Puzzle 1:

Puzzle 2. No, It's an optical illusion.

Page 74

(*top*) A cat.

(*bottom*) Turn the page upside down. Their heads are formed from the leaves nearest the plant pot.

Page 75

(*top*) They borrowed another horse, making a total of 18. It was then possible to divide them as per the King's request. The first son was given half (9), the second was given one-third (6), and the youngest got one-ninth (2), making a total of 17. They then returned the borrowed horse. Did you notice the king changes into a horse when the page is turned upside down?

(*bottom*) I C Q (I seek you).

Page 76

(*top*) 28 hours. In the 28th hour, the frog will jump out of the well when it jumps up 3 feet.

(*bottom*) ENO. The sequence is taken from the initial letters of Ten, Twenty, Thirty, Forty, etc. The next ones are Eighty, Ninety, One hundred.

Page 77

(*top*) You would need to pull out 3.

(*bottom*) The hero is in the bottom left corner. Rotate the page 90 degrees counterclockwise to see him.

Page 78

(*top*) A B (bee) usually follows it.

(*bottom*) An umbrella.

Page 80

(*top*) Moses took no animals into the ark. It was Noah who took them.

(*bottom*) The letter N.

Page 81

(*top*) It says JULY ILLUMINA-TION, reflecting vertically.

(*bottom*)

Page 82

(*top*) A stitch in time saves nine.

(*bottom*) 1. The supply of pills will last one hour. 2. Keeping your eye on the pill, bring the picture slowly towards your face until the pill disappears in the monk's mouth.

Page 83

(*top*) You take your feet off the floor.

(*bottom*) The letter G.

Page 84

(*top*) All the red words are still readable. This works because all the letters used have vertical symmetry. Turning the page upside down flips the letters horizontally and vertically. Holding it up to the mirror flips it horizontally again, so the only overall change is a vertical flip—which doesn't make the letters look any different, since they're symmetrical in that direction.

(*bottom*) Ruth Bigger, because she's a little Bigger.

Page 85

(*top*) The numbers 1 to 9.

(*bottom*) Abraham Lincoln.

Page 86

(*top*) The one with the biggest head!

(*bottom*) It says: Puzzles are fun.